The Experience Of Being Human

Walking Through Life

Michael Alan Paull

LLL Communications, Inc.
Coral Springs, FL

Books By Michael Alan Paull

The Experience of Being Human:
(Three Volume Set)
WALKING THROUGH LIFE
TALKING WITH GOD
THE PERSON

A Collection of
Anecdotes and Personal Reflections
On Life

To Learn more about the author go to:
MichaelAlanPaull.com

Copyright © Michael Alan Paull, 2007. All rights reserved.

Without limiting the rights reserved under copyright reserved, no part of this publication may be reproduced, stored in, or introduced into a retrieval system, or transmitted in any form or by any means without the prior written permission of the publisher of this book. The scanning, uploading, and distribution of this book via the Internet or any other means without the permission of the publisher is illegal and punishable by law. Please purchase only authorized electronic editions, and do not participate in or encourage electronic piracy of copyrighted materials. Your support of the author's rights is appreciated.

For more information please contact the publisher.

LLL Communications
2900 University Drive
Coral Springs, FL 33065
LLLCommunications.com

Illustrations by Steven Left
Graphic Design by Kall Graphics: Babs Kall and Michael Wall

Library of Congress Cataloging-in-Publication Data is available on request.
ISBN-13   978-1-934580-00-4
ISBN-10   1-934580-00-7

Printed and Bound in the United States of America

FIRST EDITION: June 2007

10   9   8   7   6   5   4   3   2   1

THE EXPERIENCE OF BEING HUMAN

Introduction

To be human is to be fallible and imperfect. It is to be susceptible to the full range of feelings, strengths and weakness of which man is capable. In a strange and paradoxical way, the discovery of our imperfection is also the discovery of perfection. The means of making that discovery is awareness.

In the awareness and acceptance of our imperfection there is peace. Our humanness is neither divine nor merely an animal. It is not eternal, but, finite. It is that which we leave behind when we die. Then another and higher aspect of what we are takes over. Often overlooked and easily denied, it is the essence of living in the physical and the concrete. For some reason, our human imperfection seems to bring shame and guilt if it is exposed to our selves and to others. Its one great asset is the ability to raise questions and by questioning to look through its experience. Its singular great power is that of choice. If it is sensitive enough in the working of its spirit, it is compelled to look deeply within itself and at the same instance to look above and beyond itself.

We use our intellect to reason and interpret our feelings. We concoct rules for behavior and codes for conduct. We develop belief structures to gain control over our joys and sorrows, our passions and our struggles, and our strengths and weaknesses. In so doing, we often miss the true nature of being human. Being human means we are imperfect and fallible. At one and the same moment, within the experience of our human being, we are confronted with the extremes of our human existence. In experiencing life we are confronted with an internal prodding and an external provoking. Within each life experience there is the full range of feelings, strengths and weaknesses of which we are capable.

Exposed to ourself, the awareness of our human situation may cause us to silently cry out. In that cry you hear the sound of the finite, fallible and weakness of our person. And you can hear the spiritual nature of our person lift its voice and expectation beyond itself toward God.

My writings express my personal experience of being human. My experiences as an individual tell a story in which others can potentially identify themselves. Questions and observations about life, God, relationships and one's Self form a mosaic from which thoughts and feelings emerge.

Underlying all things are the dynamics of personal faith and hope. And, of course, the greatest energy both stated and unstated is that of love. Therefore, all three books begin with the seminal statement, "The Experience of Love."

And so, within the experience of being human, our person sings its song of faith, hope and love.

MICHAEL ALAN PAULL

Walking Through Life

Preface: The Experience of Love 1

A Long and Soulful Walk 5

Feelings 9

It's Here 15

What Will Fall Be Like 17

A Pause in the Journey of Life 21

A Pearl 25

Grief 31

The Place of Quiet Tears 35

The Meeting Place of Grief 39

Can Christ Be Far Behind 43

A Rose 49

About the Author 55

The Inspiration

A young woman was troubled. Recently divorced, she sincerely asked me the question, "What is love?." I struggled to answer the question and realized that while I felt it, I had never taken time to define or describe it. Inspired by the desire to answer her question, I sat down and in two sessions the words for "The Experience of Love" flowed through my pen and onto the paper.

Written over 35 years ago, I have found it to be a meaningful, if ultimately incomplete, description of love. Love is the core and foundation of all human experience and searching. So, it is the underlying backdrop for all of the books in the Experience of Being Human.

PREFACE
The Experience of Love

There is nothing more beautiful, nor more hard to define than the experience of love. Many things are called love, most of them limited and protracted. And yet, somehow in the searching of those courageous enough to look for it, something happens which alters their entire perspective of life. That experience is love. It is personal yet not isolated. It finds immense self-gratification yet it, paradoxically, spends its energy in giving. Words cannot introduce you to it for it is an experience, an experience between two people, an experience with your SELF and an experience with God. It is a mystery and a secret but to those who have experienced it, it cannot be contained. It is shared, it is felt, it is non-verbal, it is real —
it is love.

> Love is the expression, the communication of life itself,
>   self-love reflected and shared.
>
> Love is the majesty and complexity of humanness,
>   limited yet infinite, imminent yet transcendent.
>
> Love knows the soaring of heights and the humility of kneeling,
>   a journey through the valleys and peaks of life's experiences.
>
> Love is spent unconditionally, reckless of cost,
>   finding its value in the giving itself.
>
> Love stands sensitively connected to another,
>   concerned over the who and the where of the Person.
>
> Love is neither excluding nor possessing,
>   a mutual affirmation of self and other.

Love is not the fantasy or game of people who play,
    those pretending at love.

Love is not the romance of ego projected,
    it seeks the person behind the mask.

Love finds its object in another,
    having truly loved one, discovering a love for all.

Love is God; God is love,
    an experience, a secret, a revelation.

Love is YOU; Love is I; Love is US;
    one, then two, then more till finally ALL.

The Inspiration

In the struggles of a young man, I always looked toward the fulfillment of my life. On one particular long lasting experience, I was caught up in a walk of Faith. As I felt this long and soulful walk, I was inspired to put down in writing an expression of my feelings and my hope.

As I grow older, I have found the fulfillment of that particular journey was one of many journeys I would walk. Each was one step in the journey of life. Every stop was a part in forming the long walk of a whole lifetime. The journey of a lifetime looking forward to its fulfilled completion. The journey of a long and soulful walk.

A Long and Soulful Walk

It's on the horizon
    I see the glow
        The waited for day is dawning

Looking ahead was darkness
        No distinction between earth and sky
            Just a continuum of apparent emptiness
    For so long moving ahead was groping
        Stepping into a formless void
            It's no wonder there was anxiety and fear
                Walking blindly demands deep faith

It's been a long and soulful walk
    Filled with doubts
      and stumbling
      and hope
  Many times I've wished to stop
        the agony of feeling lost
            oft led to the deep pain of self support

But now the day is dawning
   It's not here yet
     but there is a glow ahead
     and the darkness is ebbing
 My steps are becoming more sure
        My legs are stopping their trembling
            It's coming . . . . . the end is in sight

But there's the paradox
    It's not the end
        It's the long sought for beginning
  Faith is producing a certainty
    The walking is easier
      The light is arriving

What I need now
     is the strength to complete my journey
  I need the faith to believe
    that what I see is not an illusion
  I need to remind myself
      that the sun does rise
        that night produces day

I see the horizon now
    there is a glow ahead
      the day is coming
        my journey is almost fulfilled

One step at a time
    I'm almost home

The Inspiration

The discovery of feeling is just about the greatest discovery a person can make. To feel is to be touched by your Spirit. It is found by looking within. It causes awareness of yourself and the world around you. In its finest essence it puts you in touch with love.

As a young man, I often visited the club where my sister performed as an exotic dancer. On one night in particular, I became unusually stirred by the environment of the club where the atmosphere seemed to be so emotionally charged. Inspired by the energy around me, I was moved to express what I was feeling. With a ginger ale in one hand and a pen in the other, I took the napkins on the table and began writing. The result was something which transcended that situation. I was caught up in feelings and what it meant to be able to feel.

Feelings

Have you ever looked at life?
    I am . . . . . and it's hard to see it

It's not that anything is hidden
   It isn't
 In fact . . . . . it's all there
   right out in the open

The problem is that there is so much of it
    So many hopes
     So many fears
      So many people
      So many hurts

The hardest things are the feelings
    There are so many of them

Sometimes when I look through the eyes of what I feel
    It's almost too much to bear
      So much intensity
      So little relief

When I look through my eyes at the life around me
    It seems to swirl like an eddy
      A whirlpool of sounds and sights and people

The trouble with life outside of you
   is that it touches the life inside you
  And that's another problem
    there's so much of it in you
     So many hopes
      So many fears
       So many people
        So many hurts

But the hardest things are the feelings
   those throbbing
      pulsating experiences of intensity

Of course that's the way it is with life
   You can't see it, not really
      You can only feel it

That's what a life is
   a myriad of feelings
      the capacity for experiencing what is around you
         connecting it with what is inside of you

But how can you live with your feelings
   there are so many of them
   and they're so intense

Some don't try
   they simply turn them off
      how sad
         how unfortunate

But I understand
   it's not easy to let yourself feel

Feelings are so tender
   so vulnerable
      so fragile
         so easily mutilated

But that's what life is . . . . . to feel
   Turn your feelings off
      and you slowly die
         Turn your feelings off
            and you turn life into emptiness

There isn't much choice . . . . . is there?
    Not if life is important to you
  I choose to live
    So I allow myself to feel

When I look at life
      I see it through the windows of my feelings

The one feeling I cherish most is love
    Love gives me strength
        It helps me live with myself
           It helps me affirm life around me.

I looked at life today . . . . . and I saw
  I saw it through the eyes of love
    So many hopes
     So many fears
      So many people
       So many hurts

The hardest thing about feeling love
    is that it demands to be given away

I looked at life today
    and I felt love
I looked at life today
    and saw you
I saw you and loved

If I give my love to you
  will you receive it?
    will you understand it?

Accept love
    it will turn your existence into life

The problem with life is
    that there is so much of it
  We need to taste it
    to share it
      to give it away to others

We need to learn to love
  then we will learn to live

The Inspiration

This writing was the result of the experience of a partly sunny day at the beginning of summer. Inspired by this experience of nature, I felt the urge to express what I was experiencing. It impressed me as a parable of life. The result was a simple expression of the observation of my present moment.

It's Here

It's here!
        This time . . . . . it's not almost
      It is!
    The moment has arrived
          the intermingling of the Past and Present
           has arrived like the light of a partly
         sunny day

There aren't many clouds
        but the ones that are. . .
          are ominously dark and laden with rain
    All they really bring
        is the momentary blocking out of the warmth
          of the healing light
    All they really bring
        is the impatient desire for them to disappear
        so that the light may shine

Even the darkness of the overcast is beautiful
        For the intermittent burst of rain
          only causes the air to be cleansed
            only causes the growth to become lush

The dreariness of Winter
        and the almost of Spring
          is now giving way to the full warmth
            and vital energy of Summer

It's here! . . . . . This time it is!
      All I need do
        is wait for it to completely arrive!

The Inspiration

It was the beginning of Summer and my thoughts unexpectedly began looking forward to the Fall. The question of what Fall will be like inspired me to begin writing. As I wrote, I realized that what was being expressed was my next season of life. The answer given to me was an encouraging image of a life that was full and filled. Growing older, I found it to be a prophecy which has been real and true.

What Will Fall Be Like

What will Fall be like?
        When the leaves turn
            and the vitality of life returns to dormancy?
    What will Fall be like?

First of all it must wait upon the summer
        You see . . . . . it's just beginning
           summer . . . . . that is!
        The clouds and showers and sometimes warmth of spring
           are giving way to the life giving energy of the summer sun

The Fall will become the crowning glory
        of the beauty and the productivity of Summer
    Before the Sun's rays tilt to their glancing stream
        of Fall's light
           the first rays of Summer Sun will produce the fullest
                opportunity for growing and re-creation

What will the Fall be like?
        It will be the harvest of the spring planting
           and the vital energies
               and the careful tending of Summer
    It's not strange to contemplate the Fall
      Even though summer has just begun to arrive
    For the Fall is the time of reaping the harvest
        it is the crown of life
           the gathering season
              a time of thanksgiving
                  the satisfaction of a planting well made
                the pleasure of the fruit of your labor

To contemplate the Fall
        is to look forward to the inevitable reward
                The reward of moving in harmony with God's energies
                The pleasure of the created co-operating in the
                      reproductive flow of divine creation

The Fall is the braving of the Spring rains
        Sometimes too much to be effective
            yet vitally essential
        The Fall is proud parent of the generative energies of Summer
            the knowledge of the right moment to reap the harvest
            the anticipation of the coming frost
                the celebration of the full cycle of life

What will the Fall be like?
        It will be the full harvest of a living harmony

The Inspiration

In my middle forties, I found myself beset with a common emotional experience of that age. It was the examining of my life and wondering about what had been accomplished. One day I felt unusually disturbed, so I went to a restaurant to be alone. Sitting there I felt a deep feeling that wanted to express itself. I took the placemats from the table in front of me and began to write. The words just poured out of my heart. When I finished I felt a certain relief. But the questions still lingered. Since then I have paused many times to raise those questions again. The answers have always been in God's hands and revealed to me within my own heart.

A Pause in the Journey of Life

What kind of exchange is there in a life . . . . . or relationship
    in the act of giving or receiving
      Does existence reveal a plan of ultimate meaning
        a beginning and an end forges a pathway of hills and valleys.

It takes faith to walk the journey of a complete lifetime
    to believe that love ultimately redeems
      and returns all things to you.
Sometimes it defies sense – this life I live
      Giving – forgiving – confession and aloneness

When your sun begins to set on the horizon of your life
    When the body slows to its terminal condition
      When the eyes grow dim and your skin bears its marks
        of a life soon over
      When your energy begins to flicker
        and ambition has exhausted its power to initiate

Then comes the luxury of addressing the star by which you have
        guided your life
    Has this light of Hope by which you have steered your course
      produced its pot of gold at the end of your rainbow dream

The courage to face this ultimate answer is the result of a life
    that has invested all of its resources and
      now stands with its hand extended
  Has the investment been lost
      or will it have been multiplied and now returned to you
        with all of the wealth of a lifetime faithfully given
 Or will the promised significance of a lifetime well spent
    find as its exchange an empty hand

Hard questions
    asked by a man who stands on the closed account
        of an invested youth
  A man who views the sun overhead
    and recognizes the lengthening shadows
        of the oncoming eventide

Having invested all of his resources
    he stands at the fateful step
  There must soon be a return on his investment
    the treasury of his life is empty and his next steps will determine
        whether his life is of significance or whether it is
          just the unwinding
        of a clock clicking away the end of a time

One thing is for certain
    The sun will set
        and the end of opportunity will bring with it
          the fateful answer
Am I dreaming or am I inspired?
  Is my life significant or is it the subtle manipulation
    of self-deception
  Will I have lived only to die?
    Have I really mattered at all?

Lord, God – only you have the answer
  please hear the cry of a tired body and a lonely heart
    dry my tears which are never shed
      and hear my voice which has no sound.

The Inspiration

It was Sunday morning. I was at a coffee shop looking over my material for Sunday services. Suddenly I was moved by the Spirit, "Take some paper and write about love!" So, following that familiar urging, I began writing. Out came a writing about love as the discovery of a Pearl of self-understanding. Incorporating it in my message, I read it that morning.

It exactly describes my experience and, I believe, the experience of all others who know the love of God. Love and its demand to love others.

A Pearl

I've made a discovery
        a rare pearl of self-understanding
     It concerns love
       it's about my long search for fulfillment

In the long lonely looking for someone to Love me
       I've found a truth
        a subtle . . . . . honest truth
         It's not so much my need to be loved
          rather . . . . . I need to love

I need a receptive responsive person to love
        Someone who'll become the receiving
        responding object of my love

In all my crying and pleading for love
        it was not so much what I needed to receive
     What I needed was you
       a receptive . . . . . responsive you
      to return my love

You see . . . . . I have a dilemma
       it concerns me and my God

The problem is that He loves me
       my dilemma is that He has poured His love
        into my life
         and I must give it away

Because that's the way it is with God's love
        when you get it . . . . .
                you can't keep it

It demands to be given away
        Recklessly . . . . .
                but sensitively given away

And so . . . . . you see
        I need you . . . . .
                I need someone to love

And that creates a dilemma for you
        the anguish of returning my love

My mind is clear
        God's love is not hidden
            the barrier is my inability
                to receive it
                to return it
                    to give it away to others

And that brings me back to myself
        instead to the question . . . . . "Who will love me?"
            the honest query . . . . . "Am I capable of loving others?"

And that brings me back to you . . . . .
        I need someone to love

Will you let me love you
        will you receive my love
           will you respond

And that brings me back to God
        for that's where it all began

Can I risk my love again
        can I love . . . . .
                can I ask Him to love me

And so I do . . . . . I surrender myself to Him
        I hand all of my needs of love over to Him

And something strange happens to me
        Something rare and wonderful
        I am filled with love
                the warmth
                      and power
                          and beauty of His love

And there becomes a new restlessness within my soul
        I have something to give away
                something that I cannot contain

What God has given me
        is not mine to possess

I now know what it means to love myself

And I hear the Words
        imploring me to love you as I love myself

It all makes sense
        I love because He first loved me

And so . . . . . you see I need you
        I need to love
            I need to complete the circuit . . . . . the triangle
                of God
                    myself
                      and my neighbor

I've made a discovery
        a rare pearl of self-understanding

It concerns love
        it's about my long search for fulfillment

In the long . . . . . lonely looking
        for someone who'll love me
            I've found a truth
                a subtle . . . . . honest truth

I've found that God loves me
        and out of self-love
            I love you

The Inspiration

A new friend in the Church had just lost his father. As he left for the funeral, I told him I would write something for him.

Later that evening, at a restaurant with my wife and her daughter, the funeral was discussed. "Write something for him now," my wife's daughter said. So I turned the placemat over and began to write about Grief. Never having personally experienced the death of a loved one, I found the words that I wrote and the picture it drew interesting.

When he called, I read him the writing on Grief. "Did it speak to you? Did you understand it? Did it help?" I asked. "Yes," he answered me, "it helped a great deal."

Little was I to know that two years later it would become a source of comfort and understanding to me. My 18-year-old son would be killed in an auto accident. It was the first thing I sought to read. I found it to be profoundly accurate as it spoke its simple words to me. All I could do was thank God.

Grief

From deep within the Soul of Life
    a cry utters its silent agony.
        An arrow called Grief strikes its target called Pain.

From the hand of Fate,
    a burning arrow leaves its well directed bow
        to pierce my heart unexpected.

The resulting pain escapes from the deepest recesses
    of caverns unexplored and virgin,
        now molested by the intrusion of a Fateful hand.

From somewhere deep within that undiscovered cave
    a groan of agony echoes its surprise.

Something so open and unprotected has been mortally wounded
    and its sound swirls round and round
        until it loses itself in an even deeper hiding place.

And so, the surface tears of life
    turn their attention away from that soundless pain.

An arrow is now left buried but not lost
    deep within the Soul of Life;
        its presence to be forever known as a subtle,
            untouched feeling
                which expresses itself within the heart of other things.

One day, that pain caused by grief will be gone,
    removed through a healing which only time will bring.
    A wounded life made well from the inside-out.

Until then.....that deep cry not easily heard
    will be known by its unknown presence in the Soul of Life.
    A soul made rich and beautiful
        because of Life made deeper.

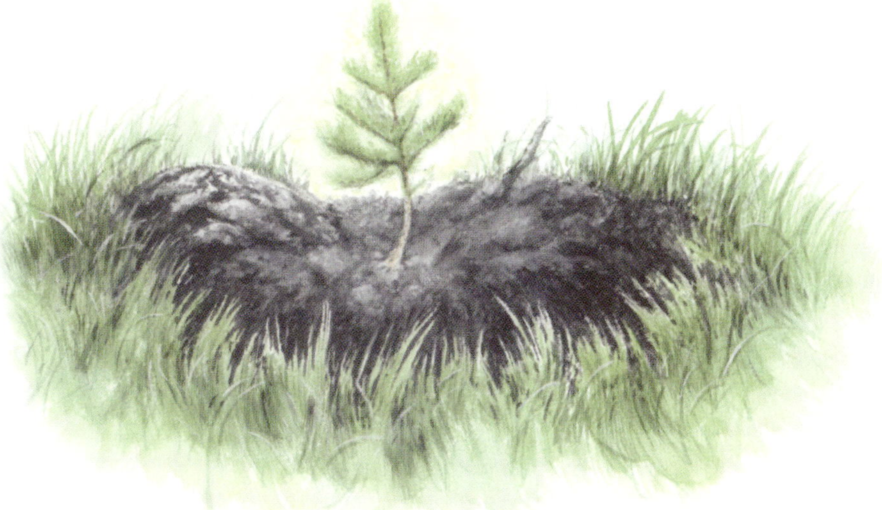

The Inspiration

On occasion something stirs in you that seems so deep and sensitive that words defy it. And sometimes, that something so deep and sensitive, struggles to express itself.

So it happened to me. For a month I ached with the feeling of walking into the deeper experience of my person. Finally, one evening, the inspiration wanted to express itself. Writing it produced the experience of taking someone into a deep place that was totally personal and where there were quiet tears. Writing it put me in conscious touch with this place myself and the awareness it brought made me feel more whole.

The Place of Quiet Tears

Come with me . . . . . if you will
    Take my hand as I lead you on a quiet journey
        . . . . . to the place where I live my deepest and
        fullest

Shhhhhhhhh . . . .
    Be quiet . . . .
        Take off your shoes . . . .
          Walk softly . . . .

Be tender and sensitive
    as we travel step by step
        inward
          and deeper
            into my person

As we walk quietly and deeper
    we must leave behind the sounds of outer voices
        . . . . . emotions which blare
        . . . . . thoughts which shout

Outer voices of thought and emotion
    grow dim as we walk our quiet journey

Soon all sounds fade away
    The stillness creates new ears

We listen to our hearts beat
    and our minds think

We listen more deeply

Gradually our hearts and minds blend together
> . . . . . thought and emotion become one

Stillness has delivered us to the place of true feeling

We have reached the threshold of my deepest person

Here we pause . . . . .
> You must wait and watch and feel
> while I alone walk through the threshold

I have reached the **Place of Quiet Tears**
> It is the place where I am alone with myself

Here:
> . . . . . I see the beauty and serenity of the face of my dear son
> as he lay in his casket
> . . . . . I hear the gentle cry of my newly born child
> as it breathes its first breath of life
> . . . . . I look into the eyes of my infant child
> as it recognizes my presence for the first time
> . . . . . I see the world around me
> - the beauty of the newly bloomed rose
> - the glory of the sunset

This place of quiet tears is a place of paradox
> tears of grief and tears of joy
> beautifully intertwine

It's a quiet place
        because the tears
            are personal
                and private
                    and come from the soul and spirit

It's a place where we experience the love
        . . . . . of God
        . . . . . and others
        . . . . . and our self

This quiet place of tears is the deepest feeling of love

As I turn and leave this **Place of Quiet Tears**
        I take you by the hand
            and lead you out of my deepest person

As we enter again the outer world
        I know that you have been touched
            and perhaps even changed

For that is the way it is when you are in the
        presence of the **Place of Quiet Tears**

The Inspiration

It occurred to me that true grief had a meeting place. The true message in the complete understanding of grief is love and the home of love is in the heart. The inspiration was to communicate how the heart is the place where joy and sorrow meet in harmony.

The Meeting Place of Grief

The heart within us is the meeting place
  of true grief
     It is where our Spirit and our human
       being commune
     It is the place where that which
       is finite and temporal
         meets that which is infinite
          and eternal
     It is the place where our higher Self
       meets our lower self
     It is the place where joy meets sorrow

     It is the place where that which
       never weeps meets that which
         is crying

The heart within us is the meeting place
  of true grief
     because it is the place of love

  And love is the experience of paradox

  Love is ecstasy and pain
     coming together in harmony and
       atonement

  The heart cannot be reached by thinking alone,
     by thinking which denies feeling

  To deny the heart is to be plunged
     into a fractured experience
       where grief is only loss
         and love is denied

Love is an energy which knows
    no limit of time and space
        it cannot be lost
            and knows no separation

Love meets us in our heart
    It is not merely thought or emotion
        but denies neither

    They are swallowed up in the unity of feeling
        and become expressions of
            that which can never be
                truly or fully expressed

The heart within us is the meeting place of love
    And so, it is the place of true grief
        where that which dies
            meets and communes in harmony
                with that which shall never die

The Inspiration

A local newspaper asked me to write something about Thanksgiving for its publication on Thanksgiving Day. Sitting at the kitchen table the inspiring question came to me. Where is Christ in the celebration of Thanksgiving? Can Christ be far behind? The words flowed freely and easily. After I finished the writing, I read it and was moved by the declaration of my faith. "Christ shall be revealed and we shall see him as He is."

Can Christ Be Far Behind

In this world
    of living
        and dying
            of survival
                and cold cash,
Where one earns a living
    in place of living a life,
Where the only thing Saved
    is face
        and past memories
            and a box full of security,
Can Christ be far behind?

In this world of the commercial
    and red bunting
        of Season's Greetings
            and green wreaths,
Where Santa wins the race with the turkey
    and spending takes place before
        Thanksgiving,
Where gift-searching outstrips soul-searching
    and the hungry still hunger
        and the lost still wander
            and too few enjoy too much,
Can Christ be far behind?

In this personal world
    of self . . . . .
        and others,
           of mine . . . . .
                and yours,
Where desire replaces need
    and is measured
        by treasure,
And distances between people
    are no longer marked
        by inches
            and feet
                and miles,
    But . . . . . rather
        by hatred
            and fear
                and mistrust,
Can Christ be far behind?

In this Natural World
    of Law
        and Providence
            and Order,
Where time has no limits
    and the hand of the Divine
        paints an intricate picture
            of love
                and beauty
                    and truth,

Where each stroke
    is carefully brushed
        to form the Eternal Mural
    of harmony
        and perfection,
Can Christ be far behind?

In this Creation
    which groans in travail
        for consummation,
Where the Visible is transitory
    and incomplete
        and finite
            and dust,
Where the Real is invisible
    and is known in the heart
        and spirit
            and soul,
Can Christ be far behind?

In this Universe
    of Worlds
        and Creatures,
    of the ultimate
        and penultimate
Where all things are ONE
    and Christ is creator
    and Lord,
        the Beginning
            and the End,

    Where the fractured is already made whole
        and existence becomes life,
            and the now becomes eternal,
    Where Christ has already come
        and conquered
            and promised to return,
Can Christ be far behind?

Can Christ be far behind?
    When He is already present and hidden
        in the Center of all Creation,
            and in the hearts of those
                who trust
                    and believe
                        and hope
                            and wait
    For that timeless moment when Christ
        shall be revealed
            and time shall be no more,
    and we shall see all things as they are
        for we shall see Him as He is.

The Inspiration

I was in my office. A young man asked me the question, "how do you write what you write?" I leaned back behind my desk. Turning my eyes upward, I told him, "I usually have a question to be answered or, sometimes, I see a picture. Like now, I see a picture of a rose bent over by the side of a road. I let that picture stay in my feelings and I begin to write what comes to me."

Later that day, I had lunch with my wife and a friend. I told them about the experience and that I couldn't get the picture out of my mind. Gathering a handful of napkins, I began to write. As the words presented themselves to me, a picture took form. When I finished writing I was in tears. The experience of a rose by the side of the road became an experience of love and I was moved. So it has been ever since then.

A Rose

I passed by the other day
        Along a path
           worn dusty by many feet

I passed by the other day
        Feeling the weariness
           of a body bone tired
              of a mind
                  stale from too much thought

I passed by the other day
        And finished my journey
           a beginning
              and an end
                  without much in between

I passed by today
        But something happened

I felt a breeze
        a cool
           touch
              of freshness

From somewhere
        Someone
            reached out and touched me
      And I walked the path
        in a new
           and vital way

The In Between became alive
  My eyes were opened
  My head lifted
   I saw

Along the pathway
  by the side
   of the
    dust
     worn
      road

Stood a rose
  a single
   solitary
    rose

Amidst all that was barren and dry
  Stood that rose
   that single
    solitary
     flower

A proud
  beautiful
   God given gift
    of the natural

But there was a sadness to that lovely scene
  the rose
   was bent over
    tired
     in the arid air

Then the cool breeze touched the stem of that Lovely
    And it swayed
        gently

It was alive!
    Weary
        and tired
            and bent down
                but still vital within

My heart was stirred
    Tears filled my eyes
        One
            then another
                and another
        Until they rolled gently down my cheek

And there
    on that dusty
    well worn road
        I paused

Reaching down
    I touched that rose with my finger tips
        Fingers
            Moistened with tears

A nectar to quench the parched loveliness
    of a rose
        by the side of the road

And then
    quietly
        with a cool breeze
            lifting the petals of my friend

I passed by
>	Along a path
>>	with a beginning and an end
>	And now
>>	with Something in between

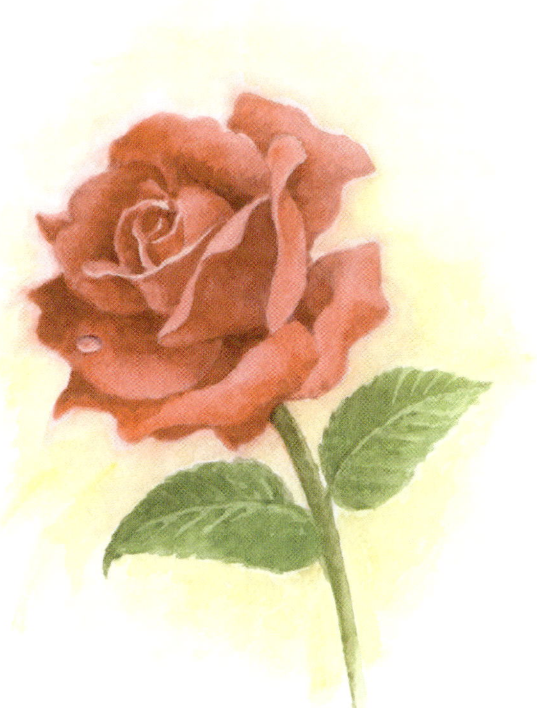

ABOUT THE AUTHOR

Michael Alan Paull is an ordained minister. Retired, he is presently focused on his writings. The subject of these writings is the human being and the experiences which make up his life. The strong belief and the core of his philosophy is that the realized awareness of what it means to be human is the discovery of the context in which all human beings, everywhere, share in common.

The three volumes in this series about the
"Experience of Being Human" are:

WALKING THROUGH LIFE

TALKING WITH GOD

THE PERSON

The several writings in WALKING THROUGH LIFE are a brief panorama of life. An experience of deep feeling and self transcendence.

TALKING WITH GOD is filled with questions and casual conversations with God. Thoughts and feelings filled with trust and hope and love. A human being in its finitenes experiencing the intimacy of the divine. A human being secure in its relationship of love with God.

The writings in THE PERSON are the introspective expressions of the self in the human situation. The experience of love finding itself within the depths of its own person and in its intimate personal relationship with another.